Gogol in Rome

KATIA KAPOVICH is a bilingual poet writing in English and Russian. She lives in Cambridge, Massachusetts. Her Russian verse has received wide acclaim in her country of origin. Her English-language poems have appeared in the *London Review of Books, Jacket, Ploughshares, Harvard Review, Stand, The Dark Horse*, and numerous other journals. The US Library of Congress awarded her its 2001 Witter Bynner Poetry Fellowship. Kapovich co-edits *Fulcrum: an annual of poetry and aesthetics*.

Gogol in Rome

KATIA KAPOVICH

SALT

CAMBRIDGE

PUBLISHED BY SALT PUBLISHING
PO Box 937, Great Wilbraham, Cambridge PDO CB1 5JX United Kingdom
PO Box 202, Applecross, Western Australia 6153

First published 2004

Printed and bound in the United Kingdom by Lightning Source

Typeset in Swift 9.5 / 13

ISBN 1 84471 046 7 paperback

SP

1 3 5 7 9 8 6 4 2

For Philip Nikolayev

Contents

Acknowledgments

The following poems first appeared in literary periodicals: "Blacklisted Titles" in *The American Scholar*; "In the Bathhouse" in *The Antioch Review*; "Death," "Things in the Morning," "My Sense of Time" in *The Antigonish Review*; "Haircut," "A Prison for an Architect" in *The Dark Horse*; "A Paper Plane to Nowhere" in *Harvard Review*; "Komsomol Act," "Christmas," "They Called Them 'Blue'" in *Jacket*; "Something to Oppose" in *Leviathan Quarterly*; "The Birth of Anarchy" in *Literary Imagination*; "Forbidden Fellini" in the *London Review of Books*; "Orpheus in the Subway" in *The Massachusetts Review*; "Modus Operandi" in *The New Republic*; "A Shave," "Dig," "The Three of Us," "Matchmaking," "Landscape with Laundering Women" in *News from the Republic of Letters*; "Gogol in Rome" in *Ploughshares*; "Tanya," "Beggar" in Poems & Plays; "Anna-Maria and the Others" in *Press*; "Axis Mundi," "Gogol in New York," "Apartment 75," "Black and White" in *Rattapallax*; "Stanzas to the Stairwell," "Golden Fleece," "Gogol in Jerusalem," "A Fly on the Faucet" in *Salamander*; "The Tale of Clear Pond" in *Slate*.

"The Green One over There" first appeared in *Poetry 180. A Turning Back to Poetry. An Anthology of Contemporary Poems*, ed. Billy Collins, Random House, New York, 2003.

Several of the poems in this collection were published in the chapbook *Stanzas to the Stairwell*, Fulcrum Editions, Cambridge, MA, 2003.

In the Bathhouse

And when at last I used to leave the house
after the lazy Sunday rest,
the sun was high. It saw a town in drowse;
a golden rush of leaves lay to the west.
All northern Russian towns are quite alike:
a river, a long street along the river,
a square with a statue of a leader
stretching his right arm forward like a guide.
The crowd headed where his finger pointed:
to a bathhouse on the river's bank.
I walked along with the others, a poor student,
a ghost of those blind alleys, nil, a blank.
In the light and shade of my sixteenth October
I carried but a parcel in my hand.
The smell of soap, of public bathhouse timber
is what I call the smell of the motherland.
And I remember skinny women's shoulders,
curved spines and—with a gasp of awe—
their loose and bulky bellies in the folds
of many motherhoods.
                              The old stone floor
was warm and smooth under their bare feet,
sunlight fell on it through the upper windows,
rays intermixed with steam and water lit
the hair of the bathing women.
Their faces up, eyes closed, they stood
under the showers, like in an ancient chapel,
and listened to the choirs of migrant birds.
With their necks craned and with their nipples
relaxed under the water, with their palms
caressing chests and falling to their hips,
with bluish veins crisscrossing their slim ankles,

they looked like water nymphs.
Time, hold them still, save them like flies in amber!
I look out of the window across the cobblestone plaza.
I see the autumn river which like a saw
cuts through the log of the horizon.
The eye finds only what was there before:
the sky, the water, many rivers ago.

Gogol in Rome

Annoyed with the parochialism of the "fantastic city"
of St. Petersburg and close
to the unexpected end of his life,
Gogol escaped to Rome.
He settled in a colony of Russian artists,
sharing lodgings with his bosom friend,
the painter Alexander Ge.
On their long walks they discovered
"the inner meaning of everything."
Gogol, a perpetual titular councilor,
was almost happy there: he could forget
the petty insults of the civil service
and a failed career at the University. He was secretly
working on Book Two of his magnum opus,
Dead Souls, stealing bits of furniture and parts
of the domestic atmosphere
from paintings of his late-Romantic friends
into the mansions and orchards
of his grotesque characters. His own
descent into madness occurred in strongly marked stages.
He saw that everything was alive in Mother Nature—
trees, stones, sand on the beach, seashells—
and everything called for his empathy.
He stopped eating, stopped drinking wine
(that blood of grapes), turned almost into a Jainist.
His friends were appalled; his mother freaked
whenever she received another of his
strange and ambiguous letters,
full of advice for the improvement of the Fatherland.
His doctors prescribed enemas, hazardous treatment
which seeps potassium out of the body,
causing a deterioration at the heart. He destroyed
his novel, throwing four hundred pages

into the fireplace, and would now spend his days
mostly in bed, covered with three woolen blankets.
"It's cold in Italy, it's dark!" he complained to his servant.
The doctors bled him with leeches until he was dead.

The Birth of Anarchy

For Glyn Maxwell

I wish we could drink that oily Arabic coffee
on the open veranda till the end of autumn.
I wish the police declared a curfew
and the waitresses sang their anarchist anthem.

I wish the wind broke into a newsstand
and dragged newspapers to the nearest abyss,
and the lights went out, and all bankrupt street vendors
left their goods at the feet of paupers.

And the wind tore into the booth, and the snow
of print settled slowly, gradually melting,
and the lights died down and glowed low—
and who could wish such a thing but an owl or a cretin?

And paupers got drunk, and policemen threw fits,
stuttering in forked tongues like apostles,
and the day was a night, and acacias' tips
were coins on fake marble tables.

Modus Operandi

The curtains drawn, all rectangles are blue.
Four morning pigeons wheel in the school glue.
I hate the treacherous light of December.
Cold. I eat pumpkin soup out of the blender.

The central heating grumbles: "You, get out."
Right. I put on my coat and off I go
where the salted red herring of the pavement
waits for the imminent snow.

Trot, trot along, you, unbuttoned biped,
across a skeleton of rusty tracks, with others
clutching in hand their steamy paper cups—
their secular candles.

March—ein, zwei, drei—under a crescent sun,
like numbers to infinity, ahead
through all the painted hallways of the town,
through all the scheduled winters of the world,

through all the bleaching mornings of the year
to where the distant clock chimes in the square—
whether to add up or to disappear
in the empire of digits, paying your fare.

A Dance without Music

Oleg from Building 4
strips off his clothes
during the morning walk
and dashes among us
with huge kangaroo leaps,
chased by two male nurses.
Say no more. Smoke.

His bluish boxers brave the nippy air.
And, finally, when almost caught,
he grabs my shoulders and holds me like a shield
between himself and them. Together we
stomp our feet on the bald hospital lawn,
while other patients and their relatives, etc.
stare in awe, yet with indifference.
A contradiction? Say no more.
It is a contradiction, if that matters,
unthinkable to Sunday morning visitors,
compatible with the inmates of Building 4.

Moscow—Berlin

When they lifted our train car into the air
at the Polish border at Brest
so as to resettle it upon a new set of wheels,
(Russia's rail track width is different from Europe's),
I experienced a moment of levitation
and knew I had left my fatherland.

We crawled through the dark winter
outskirts of Eastern Europe.

Passengers in our car, mostly
new generation black marketeers,
were sharing with each other
stories about the vicissitudes
of their previous trips to Germany.
Some gave me advice on methods of smuggling
stuff through Soviet customs
when and if I decided to return.

It was assumed that I would do
"smart things" with my money.
Russian banks in 1989
still sold six Deutschmarks to a ruble,
the then official exchange rate,
reminding us travelers
of the abiding absurdity of our homeland.

"Get a VCR, you can push it
right at the railway station in Moscow!"
whispered a well-groomed woman
with three golden crowns
in her front teeth. "Black jeans
also sell great, but smear them with chalk
so they don't look new."

Behind the windows lay Eastern Europe;
hungry children besieged our train at station stops,
collecting empty beer bottles.

We arrived in Berlin at night;
its eastern half, which I had just crossed,
lay immersed in a lucid darkness,
while West Berlin was flooded with light.

Eugene and I would often go
and wander through icy streets,
drinking schnapps in cheap pubs,
feeding on junk food and reciting poetry.
On one of the last days
he took me to the Russian bookstore "Kniga,"
where I experienced a second levitation.

The books filling the bookshelves
made me feel what some Egyptian pharaoh
must have felt within his sacred pyramid,
where no living soul could enter.
I bought Nabokov's *Lolita* and *Glory*,
a three volume Mandelshtam,
and everything they had by Brodsky.

A month later,
two minor things made my return bearable:
the paperback treasures
hidden underneath worn jeans and sweaters
at the bottom of my suitcase
and my pride at having smuggled them in
through Soviet customs.

A Fly on the Faucet

In the train of homes on this map's slope
I am a passenger in green compartments,
a nut puzzled to the marrow, forever
rummaging the drawers for a missing document.

My foreign passport, my ticket, my hands shake.
Things evaporate, keys play hide and seek,
books rewrite themselves. My favorite characters
rebel against authorial judgment.

Prince Myshkin regains sanity, returns to St. Petersburg,
Levin sells his wheat fields and takes Kitty abroad,
dear Venichka wakes and sees through the window
the unattainable lights of Petushki.

Landscape moves behind curtains,
hills roll out into a plain. Last night I noticed
we were going slower: a bookshelf in a suitcase,
the windmill of a dusty fan, a fly on the faucet.

A Waltz

A Russian accordionist in Harvard Square
plays a familiar antique waltz
and I suddenly remember the lyrics,
which have escaped my memory for years:
those warriors sleep on Manchuria's hills,
where no Russian words can be heard.

Our school's choir once rehearsed it
for a New Year's Eve performance
for hours in a big cold auditorium:
a dozen boys in navy blue uniforms
and seven girls in brown dresses
and a shabby piano in front of
empty rows of chairs.

Some of those boys now sleep on Afghan
and Chechen hills, some of those girls
sing with the angels,
afraid to mess up a note,
while the old music teacher scratches his beard
and waves his conductor's baton.

A Farewell to Russian Symbolism

In memory of Anna Akhmatova

A drunk marine snores on a wooden bench,
embracing his well worn shoes. He's taken them off
lest some local thief abduct them
whilst he is on leave from his body.
Another bench is taken up
by three lit teachers visiting from Saratov.
They smoke *Parliament* and talk
in low conspiring tones
of "she who is no longer there."
Tall cottonwood trees shed white fluff
on children's hide-and-seek
under the poet's windows, now wide open.

Outside, Liteinyi Avenue roars by,
a driver curses pedestrians, a cop
curses the driver, the streetcar track moans
as a rusty streetcar rattles by like junk.
On this side of the courtyard wall
loudspeakers' boxy birdhouses
emit cacophonic music
with white droppings upon visitors' heads.
In other words, life goes on.

I, sitting on the porch with a book,
stretch my legs over the gravel path
and eat a sausage sandwich, sharing it
with two dirty Gypsy boys,
suddenly realizing that one of them is a girl.
Life goes on,
and when I ask the gardener what time it is
I hear "Sorry, lady, I just sold my watch."

Double Vision

Trying to choose between two wooden chairs,
I choose the wrong one, a ghost.
My double vision hasn't improved.
Instead I have started
after a surgery on both my eyes
seeing shadows on a par with objects
and even more vividly. Blue, loud, violent,
they flash at me from the corner of my eye.

As to the actual contents of my room,
they have doubled their number
like creatures in Noah's Arc.
Two brooms, two vacuum cleaners, two tables,
two above-mentioned wooden chairs, a window
and a window and a window and a window.

I open a door (not the one I open)
and there's a gothic shadow
all over a rusty Christmas tree
leaning against a street lamp.
I take a step, two steps, from the porch.
A white step, a black step in the air.
Everything wears bright auras
and there is no perception of depth
between the real tree and the unreal,
between my body and its double, me.

At the Kishinev School for Deaf and Mute Children

My first autumn after college I worked
at the Kishinev School for the Deaf and Mute,
whose voices were not speech,
yet sounded like a language.

A foreign language, muffled and unknown
to the teachers. Its strange vowels,
born in their windpipes,
burned away in their throats.

I wrote the alphabet on the blackboard,
watched them move their lips as they
tried to articulate the sounds of Russian,
but no one could help them.

Yet there was a children's god in the classroom
who guided them across quicksand
to where the Tower of Babel stood crumbling
and filled their mouths with the ABCs.

Prague

For Alexei Tsvetkov

The day starts as an old man's shadow splits away
from the eastern wall. I have entered the city
on the opposite side from Kafka's K.
Locks gnash their teeth behind my back,
low-lintel doors of cafés spring open, street vendors
lay out the first radishes and scallions
on newspapers by their feet. I can see myself
being from around here, speaking their easy language,
eyeing the same chestnut trees in the humpbacked
lane as I leave my house in the morning,
shutting a low-lintel door and bearing uphill
toward the dark castle all the way at the top.

They Called Them "Blue"

They called them "blue" and mentioned them in whispers,
as if they represented a sinister cult.

This couple lived in a bohemian slum,
where most Moldovan gays rented cheap rooms.
I had never been there
until a schoolmate from that neighborhood
took me to check them out. Putting out our cigarettes,
we climbed the stairs to the top floor.

A gray haired man opened the door,
looking like a monk in a monumental bathrobe.
He made us Turkish coffee and scratched his tonsure:
"Where shall I put this?" I realized
that their place had no furniture except for a bookcase.

Sergey was a book binder and restorer of rare books
at a local history archive. He had learned his trade in jail,
doing time for homosexuality. Books were all he had.
The room's large square window offered
a majestic view of Kishinev slums. In the kitchen,
a tape recorder played non-stop, a guitar and a violin
vying with each other. Czech jazz, he explained,
anticipating my question.

Then his friend arrived, a young underground artist
with an enormous watermelon in his arms.
"I stood in a line for a damn hour,"
he cursed, "This thing had better be ripe,
or I'll drop it out the window!"

The watermelon soon revealed its green interior.
We ate it with spoons, listening to the music,
which I liked. I still remember the watery taste,
the many seeds that were left when the rest was gone.

A Komsomol Act

He was the Komsomol Leader of our class,
and I a troubled girl.
He once paid me a visit when I was home sick
and sat down on my narrow couch.

He said that I should read Lenin's works
and brush up my physics and math.
I told him to shut up and kissed his mouth
and smelled his chewing gum breath.

His embrace tightened on my shoulder blades,
his Komsomol badge pricked my neck.
I remember the ceiling growing darker above us,
and darker, and darker, and dark.

To the sounds of winter, trolleybus tinkles,
feet trotting across snow,
Lenin smiled shrewdly and closed his eyes
between our slippers on the floor.

Self-Portrait in Pajamas

Who is this sleepy, gloomy scarecrow
in morning knots of her own red hair,
who sits at the kitchen table
without breakfast?
Water shadows dance on the wall
among grape leaves.

Is she the same me
that forgot to shut the faucet off
before going to bed last night?
Water drips into the kitchen sink,
a vine breaks in the wallpaper vineyard,
soy soap melts on zinc.

Golden Fleece

I used to undertake those strange journeys
with an empty bag and a pocketful of cash,
leaving home early as the Kishinev chimneys
were coughing up their first smoke into the winter air.

The bus went from village to village across fields.
Peasant passengers slept with their heads on the their bags,
waking up from time to time for a gulp of water from a bottle
or to nurse a crying baby to sleep.

I, a smuggler with a Nabokov in my hands,
was going to buy sheepskins by the Bulgarian border
and carry them back to Kishinev, where a few friends
sewed ladies' coats from them for the black market.

Two years after graduating from college,
where I had studied language and literature, I couldn't
land any other job. This one was seasonal
and paid very little, but enough to permit me to live alone.

I liked my secret trips to the south of the land:
it was less settled, the hilly steppe more empty.
After six hours of bus time my feet felt heavy
as I walked toward a row of whitewashed huts.

I would find the right door and knock. They'd let me in,
treat me to wine and cheese and fill my bag
with tough-smelling golden sheepskins. We gossiped
about life in the capital, local life and life in general.

They knew my father was a dissident and in prison
and gave me a good discount out of respect.
They were well-to-do, but I appreciated
their compassion. They hated the Soviets too.

Once a policeman stopped me at a bus stop,
opened my bag and extracted the skins,
but the strangers around us began to shout
that I was one of them, from their village.

An old Moldovan man swore I was his niece
and those skins were not for sale. The policeman
didn't believe him, but stepped out of my path,
letting me get away with my golden fleece.

A Paper Plane to Nowhere

There was one autumn vulnerable light
locked in the transparent and fragile objects
of a mental hospital within my sight.
I took my medicine without progress,
which made me meditative but not bright.

Each day I woke at seven, ate bland food,
drank weak cold tea and walked under the escort
of a physician in an unfriendly mood
to a remote section. Here my imprisonment
became almost inanimate, absurd.

Among some loonies in the corridor
I'd wait in a silent line for the door
to open wide and let me in again.
The male nurse called with a phonetic flaw:
the stress fell either after or before,
but not in the golden mean of my strange name.

I was eighteen, morose, a little blind,
bereft of glasses after that fistfight
with a policeman. Thus I was arrested
and woke up on a rough asylum bed.
Evil regimes must kill, but understand
who has an Achilles' heel, who an Achilles' head.

Slow as a turtle after taking pills,
I walked to the "art therapy" ward, where patients
made paper boxes or "developed new skills,"
e.g. cleaning rusty irons, knitting mittens
and socks for patient nurses and impatient docs.
But I would always doze or, playing hooky,
read a forbidden book under the desk
with nurses in the background watching hockey.

Then one good day they brought a bunch of kids,
who limped, and drooled, and smiled with their wry mouths.
They looked at us from behind heavy eyelids
and couldn't do a thing. After two hours
they were all taken back. Some fellows said:
"Those kids looked really, really sad."

Another day they came again and stared
at us, the other patients. No one cared.
They were mumbling a dark stifled cry,
sometimes they touched the paper, gave a shy
and happy sound of comprehension. Weird!

They had no difference, but their clothes did.
There were skirts and pants. A female child
came close and bestowed on me a glance
of admiration in her greenish eyes.
I looked in them and saw an abyss of sadness,
the asylum of our mutual madness.

I looked into her eyes and saw my face
and yellow spots of Russian swamps in April,
a chain of golden lights, a lace of days,
while she stood still, a little ugly angel.
I made a box out of gray paper. That
was all that I could give instead
of wisdom to myself and to that orphan.
But she seemed happy with my paper coffin.

Her name was Carmen. Colorless and sloppy,
her flesh was older than her mind.
To stare at nothing seemed to be her hobby,
as well as mine.
That autumn, just to meet her expectations,
I learned to make all kinds of paper things:

planes, boxes, trains and even railway stations,
and white, white ships, and cranes with widespread wings ...
They flew and swam across the dirty table,
across the lakes of glue, and seas of paint
toward the window with its yellow maple,
whose autumn brushes always were so wet.

That eighteenth autumn, all those ugly ducklings
taught me to laugh at the slapstick universe.
Forgiveness and forgetfulness, my darling,
oh my Carmen! My life is also scarce
and made of paper.
                In the evening, nurses
would take them back to the orphanage and I
would walk across the park which mumbled verses
in the blind alleys for a lullaby.

A Wolf

Once when I was fifteen, I cleaned my room
and went to empty out the garbage bucket
at the neighborhood dump, where I found a big dog
that was scouring for leftovers
on January snow behind the containers.
When he raised its head and examined me
with a most attentive stare, inexperienced as I was
in matters of animal behavior, I was instantly aware:
it was not a dog. Whether the angel of death
or an extraterrestrial, he neither wagged his tail
nor lowered his gray eyes the way dogs do
under similar circumstances, but rather waited
for me to dispose of the garbage and leave.
When I looked back from my porch, his eyes
were still on me in the bleached air.

Another time, many years later in Israel,
I went from West to East Jerusalem
by bus, because I had to interview
a PLO activist woman for a Russian magazine.
Her hotel was not easy to find.
I walked into the wrong lane and saw a man
writing Arabic graffiti on the wall of a building.
His hand with a piece of a charcoal dropped
as he fixed me with his slow and cold
unblinking eyes. Our staring duel was short-lived.
He outstared me, and then I left.

Anna-Maria and the Others

It was a boring school party.
Two girls, twin sisters and very pretty,
Anna, Maria, danced. The others watched and yawned
and swapped teenager jokes. Some stood alone,
who couldn't dance at all. But what a pity!
I was a part of that salt pillar party.

Then one by one we gathered in the school yard
and fled to smoke a bitter cigarette.
It was past sunset, and the grass was wet.
We sneaked into an open swimming pool.
Climbing over the fence was not too hard.
The water was as radiant as it was cool.

We sat on dewy benches, had a chat.
The night above us winked, lazily spat
a star or two into the pool; its dome
lay on the bottom like a magic stone,
and linden trees strewed white nightmares.
The moon like a moonwalker went upstairs.

The twins—we simply called them Anna-Maria—
went to the edge of the tiles and touched the water.
"It is all right!"—and they took off their sweaters,
skirts and socks. It was becoming clear
that they were serious about this scary matter.
Yes, they were serious about the matter.

Anna was slimmer and more blonde, and she
splashed us with laughter, water, and Maria
swam to the other side and sat under a tree.
Two years later she would also flee
abroad with a ballet club. From our hemisphere
we watched her step to the edge and disappear.

With one long breath we made up all our minds.
We kicked off our trousers, we threw down
our T-shirts, ribbons, fears. Naked gods
we skinny-dipped in the moonlit water, so at odds
with the dark airs of the provincial town:
may hoary Neptune bless its sparkling spawn!

As years go by, the smell of that chlorine
evaporates from the nostrils, stars get blurry,
the full white moon becomes more clandestine
on the dark bottom of the pool, as does glory
for all those water-shaking cherubim.

A deep long breath, and then I'll dive again
and almost choke and faint, but then regain
myself and find the moon under my feet:
the twins in its white orbit swim with speed,
the boys keep racing in the upper layers,
and linden trees unfold their linden fairs.

Apartment 75

The obese woman who used to wake up
our whole house by starting her Subaru at 6 a.m.
has committed suicide. Snow
hangs like a set of unlaundered sheets
in the windows. When I walked into
her seventh floor studio, the standard lamp
was still on, but could only light itself,
refusing to interfere with the dull dusk
of the interior the police had already searched.

For the first time, I felt an urge to look at her face
and perhaps to see something more distinctly
than the triviality of neighborhood permits
and the mystery of suicide allows,
but her features were shut down without offense.
I only remember a chair missing its rear legs,
shoved up against the wall for balance.

The Night before the Afghan War

We raised the first glass of young wine
in the amphitheater of Khrushchev-era brick
houses that stared at us with square eyes,
as if we were already drunk as mice.

As our jaws grew numb and heads light,
we lay down on the grass, singing in husky voices
"My Bride Will Mourn Me Fairly" or "Ships Will Wait"
till our audience felt nauseous.

From dark windows, a man screamed "shut up"
and threw rotten potatoes; a pregnant woman
floated a smile; a boy in pajamas waved to us—
we seemed so flamboyantly smitten.

The seven or eight of us drunk into dust
waved back at them, wanting the last night
to go on forever like a slow train
stretching its accordion from west to east.

Something to Oppose

As the third generation of dandelions is turning gray,
I'll visit Moscow, where my father and his friends
still prod kitchen walls with their shoulders,
drink cheap wine, chat politics, grow older
than their own fathers. The great wars are over;
death does not draft us into the defense of death.
There is a domestic paradise of ancient photos,
on several of which
I'm one of those sunny spots without features
in Eastern Europe's twilight.
The ceilings are so low they make you stoop
in this early-'6os-built "Khrushchev home" type of
block of flats. On the kitchen table
I find my father's "victim of repressions"
special privileges card. Fully exonerated.
"So what privileges does it grant you?
Can you get a visa and visit me in the States?"—
"No, but I can ride the subway all day for free,
if I ever get that bored." Of Putin he says,
"Shitty government but its very shittiness
contributes to the development of political culture,
because at least there is something to oppose."
A classic '6os dissident, my father couldn't
live in the West. There's nothing to oppose there.
He says the atmosphere of freedom makes him shrink.

A Haircut

A three-storied house of limestone and oak wood
hid on the margins of a southern city.
Here they lived. Here her mother stood,
watching her kick a pebble with her foot.
The pebble was an alien on this dusty
road to her school, and it took another route.

Here she stumbled, winced and dropped her bag,
rubbed a hurt toe in a worn summer sandal.
A boy whistled . . . to her? No, to his dog.
The English spaniel flew past the girl
on flapping ears like a spotty angel.

Blue shades patched up the bald spots among grass.
A pretzel's "8" broke in her hand into two zeroes.
Here she caught up with a school friend. Here again
they separated on the narrow path, but soon
she caught up with herself in the barber's mirrors.

Years later she'd recall that shabby shop.
Its open door revealed a tongue of gauze,
the scissors' silver swallow touched her top
and bare neck with cold hope
that while she sat here, the clock, too, would doze
like the big fly on the big barber's nose.

Drowned in a big leather armchair, here she sat.
A white starched cloth slipped from a pointed shoulder.
"Cheap haircuts for boys," promised the ad
to the white walls. And thus no Samson's dread
tortured her mind or made her older.

Trimmed hair prickling her back, she stepped outdoors.
Good bye, small world behind the looking-glasses!
Good bye, old crippled clock, grey marble floors,
crumpled cocoons of towels with hairy laces!

From flower to flower, from tree to tree
she dashed to school through the dry boiling air.
Just once she stopped, looked back and waved to me,
to nobody, a guest from nowhere.

A Death

My first love died in the Afghan war,
but not from bullets, not by the hand of Mars.
He drowned while swimming in Ferry Lake.
That's why they didn't bring him back to us,
but buried him there, in the sands of the desert.
The soldiers did not shoot into the air
eighteen times, which was his quicksand age.
No drums broke the sirocco silence.
My first love died because he couldn't swim.
They had marched across the desert for two weeks,
he saw a lake, a blister on the lips
of the earth. He sneaked out to the bank
and jumped into the water. Then his heart stopped.
A water-nymph looking a bit like me
pulled him by hand ashore. There he lay
on dry mignonette and watched the clouds
marching across the desert sky.

Orpheus in the Subway

A skeptic, perfect pitch, but the worst student
in our class, he emigrated from Russia to the US
in 79 and studied the violin at the Boston Conservatory.
I'd never seen him since school,
but only heard from others that he'd dropped out
because of a serious psychiatric problem
and turned into a drug addict to boot.
In 92, trying to find out how many angels
would fit on the point of the needle, as they say,
Alex committed suicide.

Not long ago, during a visit to New York,
I saw him in the subway, alive, playing his violin
in a passage connecting two stations.
I recognized his face and yellow skin
(his father was Korean, his mother Jewish);
he was still lanky and stooped as usual.
I waited for him to finish his medley
of Russian pop songs before approaching him.

"What are you doing here? !"—"Just playing, why?"—
"What do you mean 'just playing'? I was told
you were ..." I realized that it would be wrong
to say "dead," and paused, staring at the familiar mole
over his right eyebrow. "Each blessed day
I die a hundred times," he quoted Mandelshtam.
A train went by, a crowd came between us,
separating us for a minute, but when it drained,
he was no longer there.

The tunnel's gray tiled walls and gum-flecked cement
soon filled with a fresh crowd,
and I fled with them, thinking perhaps
he didn't want to see me. This was, after all,
his labyrinth, and my life
was already complicated enough without this.
Then on the train it suddenly dawned on me.
He wasn't wearing his glasses!
Near-sighted from an early age,
he must have mistaken me for someone else.

Rainbow

How refreshing are these morning bursts of high fever
when my hands holding a glass of hot milk
feel no difference in temperature,
and objects in my room convert
to a higher degree of brightness
like sunlit sea vegetation.
Wrapped in a blanket over my pajamas,
I go out to the balcony to finish my milk
facing a Mendeleev's Periodic Table
of windows.

Last night the rain
washed out the glasses that we'd left out.
A baby rainbow falls on the recycling box.
Its spectral completeness holds for half a minute,
but then begins to disintegrate,
shedding the red, yellow and green
ingredients, and leaving a streak of icy blue
to pulsate before my swollen eyes.
When I sleepily close them,
it keeps flashing under the eyelids,
where salt and water flow,
a natural refracting medium.

Blacklisted Titles

The USSR Academy of Science, local branch,
looking like a chocolate cake from afar
with its neoclassical stucco
molding on the cornices, stood
in scaffolding before the holidays.
Women in the windows,
armed with buckets and sponges
waved at each other through reflections
of the November sky. The last day of work
before Revolution Day
was coming to an end. An older friend,
a recent university dropout,
who now served in this castle as a librarian,
had called me at noon and whispered: come,
the room will be open for two hours,
and you'll be there all alone . . . But hurry
and don't forget to bring your watch!
I put on my gray sweater to become invisible
and took the #10 trolley and then #4.
She waited for me in the empty parking lot,
and when I patted her on the shoulder she cursed,
then recognized me, smiled and sleepily
confessed that she was "dying for a smoke."
We smoked on a bench
my strong cigarettes sans filters.
Her name was Rita, she was nervous and talked a lot.
When Rita talked,
she dropped cigarette ashes around,
peppering the air. At last we went upstairs.
I sneaked into the library right under the nose
of the old monster of a guard, pretending
that I was headed for room oo,
found door number 03, the Restricted Section,
and turned the knob.

In the dim greenish light I saw
stacks of steel laden with famous books
whose authors had fallen into disgrace.
One had fled abroad, another
had written an angry letter to the authorities,
a third had simply gone out of his mind,
and so on and so forth.
All those books,
taken out of the circulation, now marched in files,
stripped of their call numbers, like prisoners of war.
Those were the days when *Lolita*,
Mandelshtam's *Voronezh Notebooks*,
let alone a Solzhenitsyn, could earn you
a couple of years in jail. Those were books
I had dreamed of all my life,
and when I touched them tenderly I touched
the velvet of dust on the jackets.
I would read two lines from a volume
and return it to its place, then
pick another and put it back again.
It was too much, "too many notes,"
too many tunes at once.
Time gone astray, the early evening
glued the hands of my watch
to the white ice of its dial. The old Cyclops
guarding the entrance/exit had fallen asleep.
I left unseen, blended
into the crowds of people going home,
waiting for buses, loudly talking
about tomorrow's parade.
It was still pretty light in the city,
but all the streetlights were on,
and red November leaves
flew in the air past neon-flooded windows,

past all the taxis lined up along the curbs,
past the open doors of hotels and stores,
past the Monument to the Unknown Soldier,
past all street lamps, going south with the birds.

Hurdles

The last time I ran hurdles I showed up
early for the competition. There was still
snow on the Kishinev stadium. Three or four workers
were sweeping it from the tracks.
I took off my coat and dress in a dim locker room
and put on my blue shorts and a white
race jersey with a well-worn number three
printed in red over my chest. Then the other girls
began to arrive, smelling of snow.
Natasha had a strong body and long legs.
When she removed her hair clasp, her blond hair
fell like a mane over her bare shoulder-blades.
Ira, a Tatar girl, was dark and had jet-black eyes.
I knew she was the best in spite of her short stature.
Even Olga, an absent-minded freckled dawdler,
had better chances than I at sixteen.
I left my eyeglasses in the locker and came out
to stretch and warm up before the final race.

Our skin crawling in the cold, white vapor at our nostrils,
ponytails . . . We looked at each other one last time
at the start, before turning into four racehorses.
The pistol awakened us, startling every nerve.
Each step was taut but light-footed. Our elastic ligaments
and warm muscles hurled us through cold winter air.
Clearing hurdle after hurdle, we knew no gravity.

When it was over I looked around and saw the others.
They were behind me. Strangely enough,
it didn't matter to me any longer.

We were tired, and our shoulder-bags felt heavy
as we walked to the bus stop, trotting on ice,
making small talk under our umbrellas.
That Moldovan February was drizzly,

but it was getting warmer toward noon.
The next summer I moved to another city
to study literature.
Are they still running through snow behind me?

At the Young Pioneer Camp

That summer day was dim, the yellow dorms
of our Young Pioneer camp winked through the fence
of rain, when the bus stopped by the doors
of the main office building, exhaling us.

Uniform white shirts, blue shorts, scarlet neckerchiefs,
we headed upstairs for our physicals,
were checked for diarrhea, headaches, chickenpox,
bad teeth and humiliating lice.

"Are you a boy or a girl?" a nurse asked me.
I blushed and whispered that I was a girl.
At thirteen I was as flat as veneer,
wore short haircuts and bit my nails.

I'd been eating unwashed fruits for a week
hoping my tests would reveal parasites
and they'd send me home. I walked heavy-footed
out of the lab and into the night.

The rain had stopped, crickets were trilling,
my roommates were asleep, a lonely lightbulb
under the ceiling lit their faces against
gray flat pillows on ancient standard bunks.

An iron frame, a mattress with bad springs,
a clock above my head without one hand ...
I opened my journal and wrote "childhood stinks"
and closed my eyes. They were full of sand.

Veronica's Secret Life

My beautiful cousin Veronica is
a nightclub singer,
a full time imitation of Edith Piaf.
She loves a man desperately for a half a year,
then hates him passionately for a month
and walks out on him without a note
in the middle of a night
to confirm the reality of the surreal.
Hopelessly young, careless, sensual,
yet a loner.

Her understanding parents keep inviting her back
to their Brooklyn house,
always packed with relatives in transit from Riga;
she isn't fond of her kin and rejects the invitation.
Unbeknownst to them, she rents
a $1,500 studio in Manhattan,
where she will inexorably retreat
"to clean her feathers." I sympathize with her escapism. Besides,
I'm in love with her fancy, messy place
where her cosmetics sleep on the sofa
next to a felt hat, silk socks, an emerald tie
and two unmatched concert shoes with broken heels.

Her current lover drives her to Boston
and they stay with me over Thanksgiving.
While shuffling maps of Massachusetts roads
in my dark Cambridge room,
he informs me that they are planning to get married
and to throw a big wedding party.

"Will you propose to her?"—"Inevitably!" he solemnly nods.
Robert wears old-fashioned sideburns and a wedge beard.
He is slim and awfully sweet, but has colorless eyes.
"What do you do for a living?"—"I am a photographer.

That's how we met, you know.
She came to have her picture taken
for her citizenship papers, you know."
There is something annoying about this "you know."

Veronica calls me from New York every time
they quarrel. "Things happen.
We stop loving ourselves
if we start spending too much time together."
He objects to her habit of bringing home friends
after her concerts. For the first time
in her American emancipated life
Veronica succumbs.

Five months later he calls me crying:
"She ditched me without explanation. Why?"—
"I have no idea." That night she told me,
"No, nothing is wrong. I'll live by myself.
I like my own life, waking late,
not emptying my ashtray every half an hour.
Today I went into the bathroom
and saw something he would have killed me for:
my panties and bra on an open book
of modern French poetry, and I rejoiced."

Silhouette

A gray winter sun moves across his workshop
with an inspection of the tools;
it glints on a tin bucket, shuns the broom,
but lingers on the rusty metal
of the mop with its mermaid tail.

A table measuring two square meters
holds a freshly crafted chair.
The old carpenter smokes
while fretsawing out of white veneer
the silhouette of his guest, a girl of four.

Then, polishing the figure
to smooth it out for her palm,
he whistles a Moldavian peasant tune:
ti-tu-ta-ta-ta, ti-tu-ta-ta tam ...
Sawdust dances in the room.

She sits down on the floor and draws
in the dust with her finger,
then takes his gift and kisses his bearded
cheek smelling of tobacco and rosin.
It's late and time for her dinner.

In an hour they will find him dead
in the same chair, his eyes open,
the sand-paper fallen from his hand,
his head on the table, the fresh black void
in the veneer being the last thing he touched.

Forbidden Fellini

The Union of Moldavian Cinematographers
had a film archive
where they showed European and American movies,
but only to members of the Union itself.
Located in a large crimson villa
built by the Dutch architect Bernardadsey
in the New Tradition style,
the place was surrounded by a handsome
wrought iron grille
and guarded from within by a Soviet militia woman.
The villa faced the city prison on the other side of the plaza.
A square "park area," scantily planted with trees,
lay in between. In winter the park
became translucent, black and white.
Two distinct crowds would often gather there:
those coming to see a film,
and those coming to see a relative in the prison.
The former loudly debated Visconti and Bergman,
while the latter stared at the snow and shared booze,
smoking self-rolled cigs and spitting.

Every member of the Union was entitled to invite
one adult guest. One evening, in late December 1980,
just a few days before New Year's Eve,
my friend Liuba, a young animation artist,
called to remind me to bring my passport
to "verify my age," so that she could take me to see
Fellini's *Amarcord.*
We met at an empty bus stop and walked
across the icy park. It was freezing cold,
the air was pregnant with snow.
The olive trees and mulberry shrubs
stood bare, waiting to be covered.
We entered the foyer;
a warm velvet dusk wrapped around us.

Liuba insisted on treating me to Champagne
in the buffet. "It's dirt-cheap here," she said,
"for the elite." We waited in a line;
nobody seemed to be in a hurry.

Soon we plumped down on purple seats
in the huge and almost empty auditorium,
and the lights went out. The film
was like open heart surgery.
Amore cordova—a deep bright wound
on the body of my life!

Three hours later
gray-suited gentlemen in the foyer
were receiving their coats.
Someone stepped on my foot; I raised my eyes
and recognized a celebrity of the season. He was drunk.
Many of them, as Liuba would explain later,
came here to drink, rather than watch a "restricted" movie.

We stepped out into the winter night.
It was even colder now, so cold
that the cigarette almost froze to my lip.
Random human shapes criss-crossed by street-lamp light
ran along humpbacked lanes as we walked
home across the town. The buses had stopped running
an hour earlier. After ten minutes of walking it began to snow.
Liuba shook her blond head like a dog and yelled
"*Amore cordova* . . ." Two echoes returned
from limestone houses
drowning in the lucid darkness.
Snow fell on the river, even under the bridge,
on the equestrian
Monument to the Revolutionary Rider,
turning the horse into a winged sphinx and the man

into an angel. It fell on government buildings
and railroad workers' homes alike,
on wineshops, buses in the bus park, on asphalt
and the glazed surface of the pond.

Crossing Lenin Street I turned my head
and saw the ghost of a bus glowing white.
I raised my hand and it stopped and opened the front door.
The front seats were in those days
upholstered with imitation leather.
The driver's strong Moldavian accent
was mellifluous as he told us a joke:
"It's winter. Two street vendors are having an argument.
The first says the temperature is 50 Centigrade.
The other says no, it's 10! The first thinks for a second
and agrees: "OK, 7 and the temperature's yours!"

Privacy

Yellow bamboo shoots stand in a pool of water
like sharpened pencils, ready for winter.
An electric mower leans black against the wall
on a bed of mud.
"No trespassing!" sounds like an invitation
to share a six-pack of Mike's Hard Lemonade
with the spirits of this deserted space.

The old Victorian house wears black curtains
mourning the deceased owner. We open the gate
held together by a rusty bar, and in the driveway
stumble on a heap of old *Sunday Times*
wrapped in blue plastic.
Death animates the most inanimate objects.
"No trespassing" sounds like "Be my guest!"

We can finally see everything
that was invisible through the dense fence:
a rain-battered rose on a battlefield of weeds
points out toward a star.
The silence seems unbearable,
but as we sit down on the high porch
a telephone rings inside the house
and the answering machine picks up
in an old man's voice.

A Shave

The figure of their story may be compared
to the diagram of a heart attack
as it starts under Khrushchev in the late fifties.
My father, a student of architecture for years,
always had his hair cut by the same Jacob,
a Jew with a long wild beard.
His barber booth at the intersection of Lenin and Pushkin
Streets was popular for its anti-Soviet
atmosphere. When my father got his first architect job
at the Civic Planning Institute, he helped Jacob
to get hired as an Institute barber.
This meant a big warm room with a great view,
intelligent customers and, of course, a bigger salary.
Jacob even trimmed his intimidating beard
by an inch and a half as a gesture of gratitude
to my dad, who was responsible for the whole enterprise.
When five years later, under Brezhnev,
my father got a promotion, Jacob too was promoted
to become the Institute's chief barber, and was requested
to hire three new assistants to work under him.
Jacob brought over his old Jewish friends,
colleagues from the booth. Now with the four of them
wearing similar beards over their black uniforms
of barberhood, the hair parlor seemed more like a Yeshiva.
The place again became popular
thanks to a profusion of political jokes
told by four dark figures in great wall mirrors.

There were some good days in the early sixties.
My father walked up and down the marble staircase
of the local Ministry of Construction, where he was
the head architect. His office windows on the fifth floor
looked out on Victory Park, the Arch of Triumph
and the Lenin monument. Very soon old Jacob and his trio,
again thanks to my father's soliciting,

came to work at the Ministry. The view
in their windows also improved greatly,
their wages doubled, and their beards were abridged
by four inches. Their new *salon* again became popular
for its classy style and fantastic jokes about Brezhnev.
My father's hair was starting to go gray.

Then there came some bad days, in the late seventies.
My father was arrested and sent to the central Kishinev prison.
He was kept in a solitary stone cell with an invisible
window under a high dark ceiling, but spent his mornings
doing work for the prison administration,
who requested that he renovate the outside wall
and a few of the offices. He was an architect after all.
In 1980, Jacob too was arrested. He became a prison barber,
shaving criminal heads and beards. Like my father,
he had lost almost all of his own hair
and wore a number on his back—a big black 17
painted on a square piece of cloth and sewed upon
his new blue uniform. When they met again,
they didn't talk much, a guard watching them
through the open door. Jacob gave my father
a very gentle shave, and they shook hands.
There were good days and there were bad days.

The Smell of Salt

As we stand in the bright wooden chapel
I look around and recognize
Iskra's friends and relatives. There are a few *babushkas*
I have never seen before, who must have come
to Levine's Funeral Home today
for a rehearsal of their own departures.
They never miss a chance to attend a freebee.

I say goodbye to my sixty-seven year old friend.

A short, plump Winnie-the-Pooh of a lady,
Iskra Kogan
lies with lilies on her high forehead.

The rabbi spins out a complex speech
praising my friend's great gift for relating to people
and her role in the Russian Jewish community.
His sharply inflected tones are detached,
a clever smile curves his mouth.
But I know that Iskra was a loner,
her only company being her daughter
and a handful of friends.

Her life's story is simple. She was born in Leningrad,
where her mother worked in a kindergarten
when WWII broke out. There were six children in her group,
and when one cold day their parents
didn't come to pick them up, her mother had no choice
but to take care of all of them.
They managed to flee from the dying city
one day before the onset of the long blockade
and wandered through a devastated land
all the way to the Urals.
They did not return to Leningrad till after the war.

Then Iskra worked as a proofreader
at the literary journal *Zvezda* ("*Star*")
and met an aging Akhmatova a few times.
Once they even shared a cigarette on the marble stairs
of that famous editorial office on Pestel Street.

Iskra wrote poems from age fifteen,
but never published anything
and never even told her friends about it.
("I didn't look like a poet, I was obese.")
A child of the war, she craved food
more then fame. She liked to eat
and to have a good laugh during a meal.

I loved the poem she once reluctantly recited for me
after an enormous dinner that she had cooked.
She read slowly from a blue notebook,
every letter of her schoolgirlish handwriting
contained a white square: *I remember smells
better than anything else: the smell
of Neva water in the rusty canals,
the smell of yellowish galley pages
covered with fresh print,
and finally the smell
of the crude dirty salt I used to buy
during the war, when tears tasted
like melted snow . . .*

Dog-Ends

So many things have changed in my life
since my days as a student in the Urals,
when I had little money to live on,
but one vile habit has persisted: I save cigarette ends
in a can, in case I run out of cigarettes.
There's a certain fatalism in my addiction
to the burned butts that populate my ashtray.
I crave their bitter taste on insomniac nights,
white clouds exhaled out of the window.
My fellow Russian chain-smokers often tell me
that finishing off cigarette ends will kill me—
"It's the absolute worst." But the other day
my American doctor and friend and I
went to a bar. Automatically lighting
a short bent stub, I told her in shame
and self-dramatization: "That's what I do for dying."
But she burst out laughing and shook her head,
"As your physician I assure you
it's perfectly OK to smoke dog-ends.
They are as good as the rest of the cigarette."

A Beggar

Once, when I lived in Jerusalem, a beggar
at the corner of Jaffa and King David Street,
grimacing at the shekel I'd dropped in his hat,
told me that I had a big ego.

"You'll leave this place pretty soon!" he added
and, when asked what he meant,
drew a circle on the pavement
with his cigarette and mumbled: "See you, lady!"

I made a U-turn and crossed the Atlantic,
got a driver's license, found a job.
On weekends I drink cold Chianti,
claustrophobia cured by the gulp.

How soon shall I get tired of this
yellow tape measure of the horizon
banded around the river's wrist,
so as to fix my eyes on

the back of the earth. By trial and error
I've figured out that it's flat
and rests on four automobile tires,
driving the driver mad.

Gogol in Jerusalem

For Donald Fanger

It remains unclear whether Gogol really
made a trip to the heart of Christendom
four years before his death. He surely did
borrow a significant sum for this pilgrimage
from his religious mother and disappear
from St. Petersburg for a few
months in 1848. He was severely
depressed after the literary scandal surrounding his
Selected Passages from My Correspondence with Friends.
Many former admirers were disgusted with him.
Gogol wanted to escape,
hoping that God would "inspire his soul."

He wrote letters throughout his journey,
whether imaginary or not.
He described the beauty of the Promised Land,
praised the underground sewers built
by Roman architects in Old Jerusalem,
drew a pencil sketch of the Second Temple. Still,
there is something suspicious about these letters.
The witness seems too detached from the evidence.
The style of his Jerusalem travelogue
is more reminiscent of the Jerusalem chapter
of a nineteenth-century travel guide
than of *St. Petersburg Tales* or *Dead Souls.*

The letters, addressed mostly to his confessor,
arrived postmarked, but it was easy
to forge such things in those days,
and Gogol the amateur alchemist
would have had no trouble handling sealing-wax.
If he did visit Jerusalem, then why did
the greatest storyteller Russia had ever known
remain forever silent about it afterwards?
But if he did not, where was he?

The Tank Farm

Green tarpaulin radiates over sleepy heads,
dusty sunshine building a pyramid under the tent roof.
When September comes, the rusted bed springs
intone in a high pitched chorus.
The bitumen mixer snores like a demobilized soldier.

The bulky shadows of the surface gas tanks shrink,
like clouds after the rain. The other tanks
are subterranean, their black thick necks
sticking out here and there among the stones.
You can see ripening vineyards in the distance.

I, an assistant calibrator, must pour two tons of water
bucket by bucket into a tank through its gouge hole
and insert a metal pole to measure the water's level,
filling out volume tables in my mad handwriting,
which the supervisor collects twice a day.

Twice a week he sends a report to his manager,
who sends one every month to the local capital,
and so it goes on, until one day a black Volga
stops near my tank and a gentleman emerges,
scaring the clucky chickens and eyeing me critically.

Water gushing from the hose into an overflowing pail,
I am engrossed in a novel. As to the gentleman's reproach,
I cordially invite him to mind his own business.
"That's exactly what I'm trying to do!"
mumbles the perplexed oil and gas minister.

Diogenes

In lethargic October
worn sneakers hang from a tree,
a plastic bag does a dervish dance
in the driveway, high pitched
ambulance sirens grow louder every day,
as if trying to shout each other down.

Saturday comes,
and I sit down on the balcony, facing the rain.
A homeless man in the private parking lot
packs his blankets into a black plastic trash can.
He'll soon go away for the winter
and the trash can, his summer home,
will be chained to the fence.

Tanya

A pale long face, half shaded with dark lashes,
her eyes always looking down,
she seemed like a nun in her Soviet brown
school uniform. Throughout her school years
she was drawing on her sketch pad
under the desk while I did my best
to distract the teachers from her.
Nevertheless, they were often offended
by her "almost physical absence"
during Math, Physics, History
and all the other classes,
except for Biology. The study of human anatomy
claimed Tanya's attention.
She did poorly at school
and could not find a decent job
after graduating. That's how
she ended up working as a cleaning woman
in a city hospital.
One of the patients there,
who happened to be an art professor,
took an interest in the silent girl
whose pockets were stuffed with ink drawings.
One day he noticed her sitting
by the bedside of a sleeping old man
dying of cancer. She sketched
the sinewy wrinkled hands
spread on a bluish hospital sheet.
The professor urged Tanya
to apply to the College of Art,
which she did. She attended for a while,
but never graduated
because she was bad at verbalizing her thoughts
in "all those damn theory papers."
So she dropped out in 1983
and two years later emigrated to the USA.

I stopped hearing from her then,
as if her inner reticence
had turned into absolute physical silence.
When I too came to America,
I could not find her. She had broken off
all contact with her relocated
ex-friends and classmates.
In 1992 I saw a drawing
in a small gallery in Greenwich Village.
It leaped from the window shop
right into my eyes:
two wrinkled hands spread on a bluish bedsheet.
The gallery's owner told me that the artist,
of Russian origin, had committed suicide in 1990.
Police found her in Central Park
on an unusually cold March morning,
frozen to death. "Then she became famous,
though personally
I had always admired her drawings."
I wanted to buy the sketch
but could not afford it:
public admiration has its costs.
I knew that Tanya herself
had never had that kind of money
in her whole life. I also knew
that she hadn't killed herself,
whatever it might look like.
She simply sat on a wooden bench,
an open pad in her lap,
drawing the naked trees
glistening white after an ice storm,
a dead fountain under a crust of snow,
black crows on staircase banisters.
She must have warmed herself from time to time
with gulps of brandy

(she had developed a drinking problem
when working at the hospital).
So she sat for hours, oblivious to the snow
and the arriving darkness,
as the temperature kept falling and falling.

A Landscape with Laundering Women
For Lisa Nold

Back in the Urals the torches of stars
burn dimly in the frozen swirling air.
People's long shadows die under cars,
rushing from city darkness to nowhere.

Up here in the Urals, where I serve
the sentence of my youth, a winter comes in fall
and never leaves, like that proverbial guest
just out of a Soviet jail.

My window faces a pier. Near-sighted water
in the lake's gray eye reflects the wooden bridge.
On Sunday women come to do their laundry.
From where I sit I see them on the edge

of the bank. Their red hands fall like roses
in the narrow ice-holes with linen shirts.
In the deserts of snow this is the last oasis
for travelers and migrating birds,

even for God himself—on one of the days
when a crescent sun sets
early above the mining town, extending its rays
to clutch at naked branches in the forest.

The women rinse and squeeze their bedsheets, shake
their wide-spread wings. It's done. The light is gone.
The landscape is dead: the bridge, the bank, the lake—
each in itself alone, at last alone.

Christmas 2001

A dry northern wind at Christmas
brings clouds of seagulls to Cambridge,
landing them at 10 a.m.
upon Harvard's stadium.
I am dishonest,
I steal my way in to run here
once in a while without authorization,
but right now I'm just passing by.

Tall bleachers to my right
across the hollow amphitheater of winter
seem ready to surrender
to snow, but there is none.

A man in a greasy Santa uniform
ambles from the direction of Mt. Auburn Cemetery
with an empty cigar box in his hands.
He sets it down on the curbstone.
 "Free. Take anything you need,"
reads the handwritten inscription
in fat purple highlighter.

The Green One over There

My half-brother had dark sad eyes, wheaten hair
and the same gorgeous skin his mother had.
He was cute and smart and innately kind,
unlike me at his age, according to our father.
Five years younger than me,
Tim attracted all the love
my father had frozen in his heart
when I was growing up.
Tim was brought up on my old books.
He did better than I with poetry,
reciting by six some "grownup" verses
which I couldn't memorize at eleven.
At eight he wrote a poem
at the back of his math exercise book
and forgot about it.
It was a love poem
with an underlined dedication, "To A."
It so happened that I knew who A. was.
The poem read as follows:
"I loved and missed her so much
that I forgot what she looked like,
and when she entered the classroom
in the morning, I did not recognize her.
I did not recognize her long face,
nor her slow neck, nor her skinny hands,
I had completely forgotten her green eyes."
It was quite a work of art, in my opinion,
but I told him that to sigh about
legs and necks and eyes
was sentimental and girlish.
He listened to me with dry eyes
and then tore out the page and threw it away
into the wastebasket.
He never wrote poetry again, but I did.
At fifteen I wrote a short story

which had some success and was even
published in a teenager literary magazine
called "Asterisks." It was around that time
that I stopped visiting my dad's house
after realizing
that everything about this boy
put me down, humiliated me
and filled me with jealousy.
I would meet with dad on one condition:
if he wanted to see me,
he had to come to my place
or to stop by at the artsy cafe,
where my older friend Lena and I
would go after school
to sip strawberry milkshakes.
One day my father
came to my school during class hours
to take me to a hospital: the night before
my half-brother had got sick.
We arrived in the middle of the doctor's rounds.
The waiting area was noisy
and smelled of urine and medication.
Dad had gone inside,
I waited for him to call me in.
Through the door left ajar
I saw a row of iron bunks with striped mattresses.
Tim's was next to the door.
He lay leaning on a big gray pillow,
a glass of water in his hand.
The doctor wanted him to take a pill,
but he wouldn't hear of it.
He was willful, obstreperous,
he pushed away the hand of medicine.
"I want that ship, that ship . . ." he whined.
"What ship?" My father turned pale

and stared at the doctor. "Can't you see?
The green one, over there!" cried Tim,
inserting his finger in the glass of water
where a green ship, a three-funneled steamer,
was slowly sinking at the time.

Black and White

Twice a year—right before my birthday
and on Christmas Eve—I climb on a chair,
fetch a dusty Adidas shoebox from a shelf
and lay out ancient black-and-white photos
from Russia on the dinner table,
noticing that the glossy paper
has collected some tan in the corners.

One day, in the year, say, 2012,
I'll be spreading this ritual solitaire
over a bluish tablecloth, and my teenage daughter
will storm out of her room, head in earphones,
look at the collection and ask with lukewarm curiosity,
"How do you get them to be black and white like that?"

The Three of Us

First I knew his handwriting. A battlefield
of his scribbles troubled me and appealed
to my eye: letters fought with each other
ferociously, commas flew like war knives
piercing the words they separated. It was a mess,
in other words. Besides, he was left-handed.

It was forbidden to be left-handed
in those days when we still wrote with ink pens
leaking in our pockets, leaving blue stains.
When he went away to study in Leningrad,
he wrote postcards to his girlfriend Anna,
I read them with her, falling in love with him.

She was a Russian beauty with a stubborn phlegmatic face,
the arch of her nose was a bit too high,
betraying some arrogance and a logical mind.
She had slow hands, nails covered with French nail polish.
She had three scars from a razor across her right wrist.
And I was only who I was at that time.

We went to Leningrad during the vacation break.
He met us at the airport and brought us to his dorm.
The winter streets were gray, and grayish was the green
of the skies. The three of us hardly talked
to each other. I knew what she was going to say,
that it wasn't going to work out between them.

They both cried. Next morning she wanted to go back.
The three of us waited in the empty airport
till they announced her flight. The two of us saw her plane
run across the field and take up from the line
punctured with red lights from both sides.
I asked myself why I stayed if she's gone.

I asked myself what we are in if we are not
in love. The two of us. The following night
I went out and lay on the snow, and my head
got cold. I saw planes, white crosses on the white.
I saw a black pine tree cleave the skies,
letting snow flow on my eyes.

That night we made love silently, his roommates
watching a soccer match on TV in the next room.
Then we lay on our backs under a wall bulb
and talked about our life in Kishinev where we came from,
it was warmer there, more sun and bright colors
even in winter. The south is the south, he said.

Then we moved from his dorm to live with his friends.
We were skinny and could sleep on a narrow couch
in a niche, behind a curtain where their baby slept.
We loved the baby, and the room was like a palace.
We helped his dissident friends write political texts
and distribute leaflets against the Soviets.

They arrested us very soon, deported me to my town,
where I was treated gently in the asylum,
while he was treated badly in Petrozavodsk,
then thrown out of the country to the West.
Anna got married, gave birth to a daughter. I doubt
she ever learnt the truth. But could I care less?

The Rattle

Poor and nonchalantly happy
in our one bedroom apartment
facing a shabby ghost-house,
we miss
the irony on our friend's face
when she claustrophobically minces in
from the cold in her black custom-
tailored overcoat.

A nouvelle riche San Francisco Chinese,
she brings our one year old daughter
a sky blue box from Tiffany & Co.
But the pure silver musical dumbbell
quickly loses the child's attention
to a bowl of raspberries on the journal table.
Plaster flakes from the wall,
and it snows behind the window.

Our fleeing visitor, who seems suddenly
overwhelmed by flashbacks of
her own "Dostoevskian" childhood,
will never guess my secret:
I stole these ridiculously expensive berries,
our daughter's favorite,
from the supermarket in the morning.

Painting a Room

For Irina Kendall

Here on a March day in '89
I blanch the ceiling and walls with bluish lime.
Drop cloths and old newspapers hide
the hardwood floors. All my furniture has been sold,
or given away to bohemian friends.
There is nothing to eat but bread and wine.

An immigration visa in my pocket, I paint
the small apartment where I've lived for ten years.
Taking a break around 4 p.m.,
I sit on the last chair in the empty kitchen,
smoke a cigarette and wipe my tears
with the sleeve of my old pullover.
I am free from regrets but not from pain.

Ten years of fears, unrequited loves, odd jobs,
of night phone calls. Now they've disconnected the line.
I drop the ashes in the sink, pour turpentine
into a jar, stirring with a spatula. My heart throbs
in my right palm when I pick up the brush again.

For ten years the window's turquoise square
has held my eyes in its simple frame.
Now, face to face with the darkening sky,
what more can I say to the glass but thanks
for being transparent, seamless, wide
and stretching perspective across the size
of the visible.

Then I wash the brushes and turn off the light.
This is my last night before moving abroad.
I lie down on the floor, a rolled-up coat
under my head. This is the last night.
Freedom smells of a freshly painted room,
of wooden floors swept with a willow broom.
and of stale raisin bread.

Stanzas to the Stairwell

Here is the stairwell where my shadow lives,
where I smoke inexpensive cigarettes,
where a plastic lion will never catch a kangaroo
in the sand-filled ashtray on the landing.

The stairs in a fresh makeup of blue paint.
The sixth step wears a brown birth mark.
The cement remembers legions of rubber soles—
thank God no one goes barefoot nowadays.

This whole space explodes like an alarm clock
when guests are being buzzed through the front door.
The ramshackle walls can barely hold the ceiling,
but support my back reliably enough.

Come and sit with me here on the stone floor,
like the Biblical Joseph in his dry well,
in this vessel of smoke, where splitting echoes
cascade along Euclidean railings.

Be a guest of honor in my stairwell.
Sit down, unfurl this atlas of emptiness.
Loneliness is a mysterious disease.
Nothing cures it better than a blank wall.

Twelve Sheep

When I lived in Israel, I would see Bedouins
out of the car window and ask myself:
"Who are these people? Are they real?"
They were always camping far
from the central roads. Their tents and bonfires
would suddenly appear like a mirage
in the desert near Bersheva and in the valleys
along the Dead Sea in Qumran.

One windy February night, our engine died
as we were crossing the steppes of Caesaria.
My friend, a Russian physician,
cursed his Chevrolet loudly
and helped me out of the smoking vehicle.
"There is no triple A service in the Promised Land,"
complained Michael. "We'd better find some Bedouins
before we freeze to death. They've got to be
nomadizing around here, according to the atlas."

We walked two miles downhill,
wading through slimy grass and stumbling over boulders,
and saw a fire built on stones, a tent under an acacia tree
and a herd of sleepy sheep in the shrubs.
Three animals moved forward,
munching with their lips. A young shepherd in blue jeans
and a sweater emerged from the tent
with a clay bowl in his hands
and invited us to "be seated," pointing
at large boulders, warm from the fire.

A long night lay ahead of us. The Jews
slept many miles to the north, the Arabs
to the east. We sat down and talked to the Bedouin boy.
His name was Taha, age eighteen, a shepherd since age five.
He had a fiancée in a neighboring village
whom he had courted for two years.
"Why haven't you married her yet?"—
"Too expensive," he replied.
He had no sheep of his own yet
to pay for the bride, and she was worth twelve—
another five or six years of work.

Taha and his girl could meet only secretly,
under the supervision of his sheep.
Their kisses were brief (his decision:
he was afraid to lose control over his body).
His craving for the girl was torturous.
Though his family wasn't poor, his father
insisted that Taha work to raise the bride prize.
The girl's family wasn't poor either,
but they were ready to wait till he could pay.

The sheep surrounded us closely toward dawn:
they wanted to sleep near the fire.
Sometimes there were gusts of wind,
and I could smell burned wool. The three of us also
dozed off between small talk. Taha's tanned face
was the first thing I saw in the morning. "Can you
write for me the numbers from one to twelve?
Sometimes to fall asleep I count my future sheep."

Rendezvous on Sand

Stiff wind rips remnant chimney smoke to shreds,
invades the dark porch, fumbles with the door-bolt,
lets itself in, ruffles up your empty bed,
announcing how you are loved far beyond
these walls, in a new world where now your soul
concludes the concept "wind" cannot be found
in the vernacular, nor in the sagging sails
still at full mast on vessels run aground.

Your breathing quarters no longer limited
by sand, but by the edges of the sky,
this fresh ebb steals the sea from under your toes
and pauses as millennia go by,
while memory, as swift in backward race,
trips on the very spot where once the sand
bore the clear imprint of your shoulder-blade
and yet recovers no such sunlit place.

Totaled

I followed him to the West, where he shaved his head,
walked barefoot in his back yard, talked to the cold.
Autumn was in our lungs, breath visible in the dark.

He talked to the cold in German, set up a yard fire,
tossed in his photographs, bills, driver's license,
looking boyish with ashes on his cheeks.

Then one night, drunk and flamboyant,
he took me for a driving lesson in his rusted Ford.
We hit curbstones, lampposts, gates.

We laughed like crazy when the car was totaled.

Things in the Morning

For Ellen Barry

Somebody from the past, as in Chinese predictions,
calls after New Year's Eve.
The year is still so young in the Victorian mansion.
Then you squeak up the stairs.

A bright red drifting float, the sun disc bobs forever
there, in the winter sky.
And you pick up the phone. Gosh . . . Not at all . . . I promise . . .
Will see you soon. Good bye . . .

No past is real at 8 after a drinking party.
Things sleep like guests:
in armchairs, on the couch and even in the bathroom,
survivors of the feast.

Old friendship, do not call! Do not invade the garden
of stones and bleeding glass!
Befriend somebody else, my solemn winter Eden,
I want "to miss my chance."

I shunned you and escaped in swift peregrination
your rigorous fine grind.
I'm a trashy gene of a stone generation.
And I don't mind.

Cut, Occam's blade, cut off clockwise in all three windows,
a bird—from its gray flock,
a single flake of snow—from all the winters
when I was missed.

My Sense of Time

The three conditions of classical drama
are fulfilled. There is a season for sowing
seeds, stones, drachmas and words
in a little yard with a bamboo backdrop
where it's my turn to do the weeding now
in this unity of place, time and action.

This is my second life after all.
I have inclined the hourglass toward the fall,
turning the furry sky upside down,
and now see a fresh moon at my feet
confined to a puddle.

Let this be my new old house
with wet paint on the walls of the world.
Wait till rain cleanses
the ground of its latest signs and imprints.
For she lives best who doesn't know
where she is from or where to go,
but makes ends meet in the end.

I'm a woman of thirty. I look older.
Mirror rain puddle, I take no offense!
There is a season for a woman's face
to turn to a different sort of landscape.
There is a time to settle down,
because everyone settles.

Rain. The bamboo whistles about
a woman in a rustic prickly sweater
who sat on a porch, ate a peach, felt better
at the end of the 20th century, watched a cloud,
planted the peach stone
and was gone.

Camping in Buzzards Bay

Cracks in the air turn into black swallows,
seagulls dig in the silted seaweed.
As we drive up, the dunes shudder,
the bleached hair of bulrush stands on end.
Rain switches off the sunlight.
At first there's nothing but a few rotting fisher nets,
then boys with bucketsful of clams,
and finally a boat bearing southwest.
"Let's to the village and find some food!"—
"We're a good catch for mosquitoes!"
Meanwhile the boys cross the grassy ridge
in salty rubber boots.
Sometimes a night is just a night.
Sleeping bags move from love like dunes in the wind.

The Law of Perspective

Two broad orange lines of maple trees
intersect in the distance. A boxy school bus
returns kids to homes
until one autumn they disappear from view
into the word "perspective."
What lies beyond its focal point is obscure,
a spy hole of the TV helps fill
their absence with a dozen clichés. What's really there?
Future is the past projected onto the white page
with the addition of the auxiliary "will."
Pizza, relationships, Latin, cash, weed,
vacation in Switzerland, hitchhiking
on the outskirts of Madrid, and so on.
But two are dead and one is missing—
a yellow marker of the autumn light stipulates it.
Our fat red Webster falling apart
suggests, among other meanings of "perspective,"
the art of picturing objects (lives?) in such a way,
e.g. by converging lines (of maple trees?),
as to show them as they appear to the eye
with reference to the relative distance (in years?).

The Tale of Clear Pond

Once again we've settled down in the center of Moscow.
Leaving the house, we slip the key under the rug.
We buy our food at the little street market—
grapes, tomatoes, white cheese. Wine is cheap. Bread is dark.
The level of local life is low,
the ruble falls every day, and the same
can be said about the sourdough
of the clouds with the yeast of a long Russian rain.

Grapes! Tomatoes! White cheese! —salesmen yell. A door
    yawns.
Clear Pond, when it frowns, distorts our faces.
Clear Pond, where are your brown ducks and white swans?
Now we look from the bank at a crow that chases
its white shadow below in the wrinkled copper mirror.
Something is rotten in this city. But look,
the only one crying over the past is the weeping willow
bent over a muddy brook.

We once were a flock on these wet wooden benches,
but we left our nests and drifted astray.
Yet since the earth is round, the meridian trenches
have come a full circle in this rainy May.
The city has called us home for a season. And while the rain
    lingers
at the doors, we rustle our notebooks, call old friends,
shuffle days as trees shuffle leaves in their crooked fingers,
looking forward to other lands.

The Dig

In my teens I worked as an archeologist.
All summer we dug into Scythian burial mounds
for big-bellied vases of red clay, for patina-painted coins
and bronze arrowheads that had pierced many hearts.
We looked especially for beads and gems
from the torn necklaces of Scythian women.
We soaked our finds in chloric acid
and cleaned them with brushes and sponges,
then left them in the sun to dry.
The arid August had drained our water supplies.
We bathed in and drank from a shallow lake
and bought produce from the peasants
working on the vineyard across the road
in their bright satin shirts and dresses.
We, in faded T-shirts and jeans, would
in the evening pool our funds,
cigarettes, black tea and coffee beans,
and trade them for bread, goat cheese, purple
bull's-heart tomatoes, several kinds of grapes
gleaming on rough peasant palms,
making them look like roaming barons of the land.
We were young and hungry, stuck-up city kids
in the ancient Scythian fields of Moldova,
hunting for beads of time's torn necklace.
When we sat barefoot on the lake's bank,
eating and then rubbing ancient dishes with sponges
or simply wet sand, we knew we had lived here before.
When we had run out of everything we could
trade for life, the peasants sent us a gift.
Two young boys came with a basket of provisions.
They didn't speak our language, we didn't speak theirs.
We emptied the food out on big red clay plates.
Then came our last day. A rattling van stopped
by the camp. The two boy messengers
came to say good-bye, and all other folk

simply stood and watched as we loaded
crates of Scythian goods, packed our rucksacks,
put out the fire and took off.
I saw disappearing one by one
the village, the site, the silent group of peasants,
the lake bank and the lake itself.
I fell asleep I dreamed that all the treasures
in the crates had turned to grapes.

A Gentle Hibernation of Lovers

We no longer talk to each other.
When a continental October wind chases leaves,
plastic bags and bluish feathers of smoke,
we tell no fables and share no family stories.
My mother knits in a dull rocking chair,
my husband prepares tomorrow's lecture,
I mind my late vegetarian dinner.

My mother can ask me only domestic questions
and is always generous with advice.
The current topic is Greek salad:
"Did you add olive oil, apple vinegar, basil?"
This kind of discourse, based on
existential trifles, violates no privacy, but
sometimes I feel like dropping the genre
in favor of something more confidential.

I no longer speak to our neighbor next door,
who studies anthroposophy and law.
All he cares about is whether
I *really* love Soloviev, that Russian Aquinas,
and what he *really* thinks of the concept of freedom.
I answer, freedom as an evolutionist myth—
"we originated from apes, so let us all love each other"—
is not freedom. I find no common language with the scholar.

I'd like to talk to my daughter, who seems to be
straightforward and light in her motivations,
but she has just turned eleven months old,
and our conversation falls short of a cognitive point.
"Pumpkin, where's your orange ball?" I ask.
She listens diligently, grabs my shoe, bites it
and says: "Bunny, my bunny. Papa."
We have eternity ahead of us to talk.

I talk in my sleep, my husband says.
Last night I caught the tail of a long sentence.
I had dreamed of a locked iron case,
a willow tree and a black starling's nest.
"These are the three main symptoms of emptiness,"
I heard myself say and was
immediately awakened by my own voice.
I didn't risk going to bed again and stayed in the kitchen
until the night evaporated.

It's a pity that we no longer talk till dawn,
that we indulge in gentle hibernation,
betraying the feasts of conversation. It's
a pity that we open a book and yawn,
and from then on
the only exchange we can count on
is a good-night kiss.

A silly sky falls on the wooden house
like a piece of cloth on a cage with birds.
What did I mean to say? I keep forgetting words,
I grow silent and thirsty, I seal my mouth
with a cup of sweet Lipton tea
with a moonlike lemon slice.
Good night, my love, sleep tight, good night.

Matchmaking

Those schist slabs were gold-smooth and a floating beacon
shone on convex water. Our clothes were dust and sea.
"Let me talk to him," my classmate said. We walked in circles
around the ruins of Hersones,
left on the Black Sea coast by ancient Greeks.
That June we lived in summer camps, working on a dig
with local archeologists. Another work day over,
a million poppies glowed red around us in the dusk
We sat down on the remains of the Northern wall
and I answered, "It won't change a thing."

I had been in love with a boy for a few years
and never told anyone, but she said,
"We all know how much you suffer. Let me try to fix it,
I'm good at this." She had already "set up"
eight other kids. "Look, Lenka is with Stasik, the other Lenka
is with Serge, Igor is with Yulia, and Tanya is with Vic.
It works!"—"I know," I said, "but in my case it won't work."
Anyway, I was too weary of the love fever. I let her convince me.
And immediately—wasn't that a sign? —
an invisible choir filled the amphitheater
sealed by a fallen sky. Angels? No,
a brigade of young pioneers marching uphill
in double file toward the dorms.

Twenty five years hence,
I'm still grateful to my naïve matchmaker
for that gulp of hope, the happiest night in my teenage life.
How can I tell you, my long love, my skinny fawn?
I had a dream that night, and in that dream
we cuddled naked among the poppies,
and on the seashore your suntan merged with mine.

In the morning I buckled my sandals
and walked into the canteen. He sat at the far end
of an infinite plastic-covered table, eating a sandwich.
White milk had left a mustache on his upper lip.
Our eyes met for a moment, he shook his head no.

Gogol in New York
For Philip

Afraid of the chthonic dragons of his dreams,
he takes a two-horse carriage in Central Park
to go to Brooklyn to a gourmet store
recommended by a friend in St. Petersburg.
After two hours of circling around the Park,
the carriage returns to where it started.
Surprised and angry, Gogol shuffles a deck of dollars.

He appreciates the New Yorkers though. Young men
still looking like men, and young women
also looking like men. He likes
Buddhist monks for their saffron silks,
Catholic clergymen for their white collars
and black cassocks. Naval officers
in their white uniforms and blue service caps
make him amorous and happy.

He sympathizes with the local population
while elbowing his way through Harlem,
still hoping to reach that famous deli.
He stops to buy a Coke at Seven Eleven,
quenching his thirst for bitter Russian lemonade.
He dulls his nostalgia, his pricks of conscience.
He is still hungry, listens to the music
in his intestines and turns most decisive
about making it to Brooklyn.

At 11 p.m. Gogol folds his black umbrella.
Manhattan is still around him.
He devours clams at an Italian restaurant
and washes them down with white wine.
It's getting dark and cold outside,
but the darker the street, the lighter the skies above it.
Alas, everybody speaks English here.
He knew that people spoke English in New York,

but not to this extent. He is mesmerized by the fact.
He needs someone to talk to at this hour,
he needs a Russian at this point in life.
Perhaps he'll find one or two in Brooklyn,
if only he could find his way there somehow.

The Rat

Leaving the house for an appointment with the dentist,
the first thing I saw was a dying rat.
It lay on the curb near the hydrant,
going through the shakes. People walked by,
nobody paid attention to it, only I stared.
Because, you see, as much as I'm afraid of
these animals, I suddenly felt sorry for the damn thing,
it wasn't even an adult rat,
just a baby one: its silver fur was almost transparent,
and the pink skin could be seen through it.
Exterminators had done something in the building
several days ago; they had probably put some
poison in the basement. Its friends and relatives gone,
the thing was dying alone in the freezing light.
My heart pounded and my feet
grew heavy as I dragged them from the porch.
I said to myself: "You didn't get any sleep last night,
because of the toothache, and now it's just nerves."

I looked back several times,
hoping the rat would come to its senses and crawl away,
and when it didn't, I decided to examine the road
on my left and check whether drivers could see
the rat crouching on the edge of the sidewalk.
At first, the road was empty, but soon a rattling blue Honda,
appeared in the distance. As it approached us, me
and the dying rat, I recognized my ex-husband
behind the wheel. He also saw me, frowned and roared on
down Harvard Street. I hadn't seen him for almost
two years and knew immediately
that he was still sore from our divorce. That made me
walk faster without turning my head. A dying rat
and an ex-husband in pain—more than enough
for the first three minutes of a walk.

In the dental clinic they told me I had missed
my appointment. "But I'm only ten minutes late!"—
"Ten minutes and two days, to be precise," said the girl.
She was sorry she couldn't help. I had misheard the date
on the telephone, mistaken the seventeenth
for the nineteenth. I made another
appointment and left the clinic, but instead
of going straight home decided to visit a coffee place.

I walked to the coffee place and couldn't
stop thinking of the rat and of my ex-husband.
Why did it have to be so? It was his fault
that he was bitter and stubborn. But it was I
who had left him, after all.
I sat at an outside table, a paper cup in my hand,
trying to write something. ("Perhaps this will cure me . . .")
My tooth started bothering me again,
but this time I almost welcomed the pain—it was so real
compared to my access of love and guilt.
I realized that I was freezing,
that my bare hands and my feet in my new summer shoes
were freezing. According to the clock on the arch,
I had sat at the table for two hours. A big
gray cloud had swallowed the sun and hung
heavily over the street. Others had gone inside
to find warmth and refills,
but I remained outdoors. The lights came on.

"Is anyone using this chair?" I heard a voice
and turned my head expecting to see
a blind person with a stick and perhaps a guide dog,
or else why would anyone ask such a question?
But I saw a young couple
not bothered by the imminence of rain. Their lit cigarettes
reminded me of us in our twenties:

withdrawn from everything,
almost saddened by the burden of love,
rendered helpless by its power.
"No, no one is using this chair."

The Summer Gardens

In the Summer Gardens of St. Petersburg
Lombardy poplars shed cotton on our heads.
The twelve Roman Emperors along the walkway fidget
in the green shadows, a toddler god with a fish in his hands
pees in the bushes, contemplating the sky.
It's a white night.

At the Solstice Poetry Festival
We sit at an outside table of a literary café,
drink sour beer and listen to Russian poets.
When they ask me to read, I hesitate, but then say
 "But please, no microphone."—"But why?
It's a democratic country!" laugh the Russians.
When I start reading I realize I cannot beat
the megaphones in the distance at their own game.
Very soon a squad of the special police force
surrounds the café.

"We demand to be arrested!" rejoice the Americans.
Eager for fresh experience in a strange land,
they are glad to challenge the authorities
by participating in an unsanctioned reading. "Where is
the promised freedom of speech in Russia?"
I feel silly when I beg them
to obey and leave with me. "Dura lex sed lex,"
laughs Cicero as I exit
and winks to me from his dilapidated podium.

Hemophilia

Hemophilia running in my family,
a simple paper cut can be lethal.
A convert, a bookworm, a Jewish mutt,
I've left my bloody fingerprints
all over the books of others.

Today as I open a random page
two blueberries slip from my thumb
and swerve across Chekhov's lines:
"The air one breathes is gloriously soft"
and "He took a stroll down Petrovka Street."

Strictly between you and me,
this is just what Russian literature does:
it cuts the skin, makes us bleed,
it seeks our death, and when we die,
it shines through the bloody mess.

Axis Mundi

Looking like a gothic angel, which he was,
with white limestone powder in his hair,
he stepped with a cigarette after work
out of his dusty sculptor's studio,
the wind vacuuming his coat.

Still thinking of the Axis Mundi—
the round cast iron block growing
out of the floor of the Church of the Holy Sepulcher,
which he had seen in Jerusalem—
he walked across the snowed-in parking in Lynn
and freed his battered Subaru from under the snow,
his freezing hands beginning to disobey.

It was snowing crows and jackdaws.
He slowly drove along the seashore, where
finding the other end of the Axis
made a lot more sense somehow—and there it was,
black as the lower part of an ancient lamppost
next to a sleepy policeman.

Generation K

There is one lucid dream with open eyes:
I lie down on the floor, the ceiling a stage,
and see us gently floating, white on white,
or hanging still like bats in Plato's cave.

We all adore loud colors, drink on the stairs,
smoke too much and speak too loudly,
drive ramshackle cars with broken gears
from hill to valley.

We mumble in English with a heavy accent,
dropping the articles like cigarette ashes,
and suddenly forget at the end of a sentence
its initial station.

We don't really care what clothes we wear
and still enjoy French movies for their smack
of sexuality. We raise the collars
of our raincoats, turning our backs

on a stray foreigner finding a hotel
in the dark capital where we stay as guests
until we transit to a better world
as painlessly as moving to the West.

Printed in the United States
23089LVS00001B/157

9 781844 710461